The Splendors of
BYZANTIUM

The Splendors of BYZA

NTIUM

BY DOROTHY HALES GARY

TEXT BY ROBERT PAYNE

A Studio Book   THE VIKING PRESS   NEW YORK

First published in 1967 by The Viking Press, Inc.
625 Madison Avenue, New York, N. Y. 10022

Published simultaneously in Canada by
The Macmillan Company of Canada Limited

Library of Congress catalog card number: 67-25919
Printed in Italy

SAILING TO BYZANTIUM
W. B. Yeats

That is no country for old men. The young
In one another's arms, birds in the trees,
—Those dying generations—at their song,
The salmon-falls, the mackerel-crowded seas,
Fish, flesh, or fowl, commend all summer long
Whatever is begotten, born, and dies.
Caught in that sensual music all neglect
Monuments of unaging intellect.

An aged man is but a paltry thing,
A tattered coat upon a stick, unless
Soul clap its hands and sing, and louder sing
For every tatter in its mortal dress,
Nor is there singing school but studying
Monuments of its own magnificence;
And therefore I have sailed the seas and come
To the holy city of Byzantium.

O sages standing in God's holy fire
As in the gold mosaic of a wall,
Come from the holy fire, perne in a gyre,
And be the singing masters of my soul.
Consume my heart away; sick with desire
And fastened to a dying animal
It knows not what it is; and gather me
Into the artifice of eternity.

Once out of nature I shall never take
My bodily form from any natural thing,
But such a form as Grecian goldsmiths make
Of hammered gold and gold enamelling
To keep a drowsy emperor awake;
Or set upon a golden bough to sing
To lords and ladies of Byzantium
Of what is past, or passing, or to come.

The Splendors of
BYZANTIUM

O sages standing in God's holy fire
As in the gold mosaic of a wall,
Come from the holy fire, perne in a gyre,
And be the singing masters of my soul.
Consume my heart away; sick with desire
And fastened to a dying animal
It knows not what it is; and gather me
Into the artifice of eternity.

So the poet William Butler Yeats spoke of the majestic artifices of the Byzantine masters of mosaic, who painted walls with colored glass and stone and gold leaf and by some strange alchemy of light and substance produced an art so vivid and enduring that even today the walls sing and we warm ourselves at the holy fire. Paintings fade when they are made of paint, but these paintings were made of harder color than paint, and they had a deeper glow than paint can ever have. These mosaics are as nearly eternal as anything that can be made by human hands. Hammered into the walls, they last as long as the walls stand. Under the Byzantine emperors they became "artifices of eternity," the enduring gates through which earthly men could contemplate the heavenly vision.

On the walls of their churches, on domes and half-domes, around windows and in obscure corners the brilliant masters of mosaic painted the likeness of God, the starry firmament, the waters of the deep, the history of earth and heaven, and the story of Christ. Over immense acres they described events which no one had seen with human eyes or the familiar events which everyone thought he had seen, because they were recorded in the Scriptures. They described the beginning and the end and everything in between. At the beginning God stands amid the wheeling stars and out of them makes worlds and universes. At the end there is the Resurrection, the rebirth of the blessed. But dominating all, greater even than God, pervading the entire church and dwarfing all the portraits of the saints and apostles, is the face of Christ. To this face the eye was led by intricate design, for there could be no other conclusion to the enterprise. All the colors, all the lines of force, all the shaping of the walls led to the glory of His face.

There lay behind this art a profound study of the effects of light, of refraction, and of the movement of a candle flame. They knew how light wells into curved surfaces, the varying glints of marble, stone, glass, jewels, nuggets of silver, gold sheeting—they did not limit themselves in their materials, and used whatever was colorful, whatever played with the light. These masters studied the misty brilliance of glass, the gleam of polished marble, and the way gold shimmers mysteriously as it simultaneously absorbs and reflects the light, especially in the shadowy places of the apse where the light could scarcely reach. We see these mosaics today by electric light, with its steady and neutral glow, but this is not how the Byzantines saw them. They saw them in the light of massed banks of candles, jumping and pulsating, or in the flickering glow of oil lamps with their living colors. Seen in this light, they seemed to hover in a mysterious realm of their own, detached from the walls, changing with every breath of the observer and every leaping flame.

We shall not understand these mosaics unless we realize that to the Byzantines they appeared as living presences, never still. The observer had only to take a breath or move his eyes a little, and his own movement together with the movement of the flames would have the effect of subtly changing the entire perspective, so that the mosaic appeared to be in continual motion. The light became breath and radiance, and seemed to pour out of the walls. From the gold heavens Christ comes always closer, and the lips of the Virgin move as she prays.

All this, of course, is illusion and artifice deliberately cultivated to produce in the observer a state of trancelike enchantment. In the end the light dazzles and numbs, and the observer is wholly at the mercy of those scintillating hovering presences who come crowding upon him from all the corners of the church. There is no escape from them, for they fill the air and seem more real than one's neighbor, for they are larger and more luminous than any human being. After gazing for five minutes at a Byzantine Christ, the shoulders draped in imperial blue, the brown hair falling in waves, the eyes pouring out flashes of fire, the head cradled in the golden nest of the curving apse, the everyday world sinks away into insignificance. And soon you become aware that you are no longer gazing at Christ; He is gazing at you.

The Byzantine artists were highly sophisticated men, employing many different techniques, and they knew exactly what they were doing. What they accomplished was something one would have thought impossible, for their aims were nothing less than to convert temporal space into divine space, to transform a church with four walls and a roof into a place of visions. They were concerned to form a ring of enchantment around the faithful, and then to lead them into a divine world and into the presence of the living God. The light of a Byzantine church is not of this earth; it is almost palpably the light of heaven.

Nothing comparable to this light had even been known before. Neither the ancient Egyptians, the Greeks, nor the Romans had ever built temples in which vast sheets of broken and quivering light were made to serve the purposes of the faith and to establish the existence of the divinity. They set their gods on altars or in the niches of the walls, or they erected a vast and towering effigy of the god in the place of honor in the temple. The Acropolis has in the Parthenon the palace of the virgin goddess Athena, and in the Erechtheion a smaller palace which she shared with the sea god Poseidon and the primitive gods of an earlier cult. In neither of these palaces were there paintings in the interior, which was sober and unornamented, for the worshiper's entire attention must be concentrated on a single divinity. The legendary history of the goddess Athena was depicted in the running frieze around the Parthenon, high up, and half concealed by the columns. The Christians turned the Greek temple inside out. They placed the columns inside the temple and painted the walls with frescoes or inlaid them with mosaics, changing the sober interior to one of mounting excitement; over the gateway on the tympanum they sometimes placed the most superb and challenging representation of Christ, to be seen by the worshiper as he approached the church.

Instead of a dark interior there were dancing lights. Instead of a single figure to be worshiped, there was the central figure of Christ surrounded by hundreds and sometimes thousands of figures. Drowned in color, scent, and light, the worshiper entered a world as immediate and as insubstantial as a dream.

How the Greek temple came to be turned inside out to make a Christian cathedral is a long and complicated story which can be traced step by step. But one element is missing. We do not know and can only guess when the first mosaicist first embellished the walls of a Christian church. The name of the unknown genius who first thought of painting churches with colored glass and stone and gold leaf is unknown to history, and we can scarcely guess at the nature of the impulse which led the architects and designers to transform the entire church into a many-colored icon. It may have begun with a single portrait of Christ, but it is just as likely that the idea of painting an entire church in mosaics arose fully fledged in all its maturity in the mind of a great architect, whose name is unknown and whose church has long since fallen into ruins.

The art of making mosaics was well known and could be traced perhaps to the Stone Age, when men first reinforced the floors of caves with pebbles. In Alexander the Great's palace at Pella in Macedonia we find courtyards decorated with pebble mosaics. Syrians and Romans seem to have been the first to master the art, which served to decorate the floors of dining rooms and baths, of courtyards and those fountain-rooms which the Romans called *nymphaea* in honor of the nymphs. It was a decorative art, rarely showing much imaginative power. Cupids tumbled with vine wreaths, the seasons wheeled around the flaming sun, Dionysus rode a spotted panther. For the most part it was pleasantly simple, demanding no great skill from the mosaicist, who might content himself by designing a floor made of cubes of white marble, the only decorations being a blue-gray trident or perhaps dolphins gamboling at the corners. Occasionally there might appear an intricate and complex mosaic like the great Battle of Issus fragment in the Naples Museum, which was clearly the reproduction of a painting. The earliest wall mosaic appears in a first-century *nymphaeum* in Herculaneum; it shows Neptune and Amphitrite standing together, their golden flesh set against a golden sky. Neptune has a youthful body and a gray beard; a blue scarf representing the sea winds around his shoulders and his arms. This is an accomplished work of art, while Amphitrite, naked to the waist, is a conventional figure. Already in that naked Neptune we have a foretaste of the magnificently commanding Christ.

And perhaps—for of these matters no one can speak with certainty—the *nymphaeum* at Herculaneum is close to the beginnings of Christian mosaic art. A *nymphaeum* is very nearly a temple. In such a building, in the presence of running water, the light acts strangely. A mosaic of a fish beneath the water would seem to move, and so, too, would the figure of Neptune on the walls, caressed by the continually moving reflections of the water. In this way men may have learned the astonishing power of mosaics to give the illusion of movement and life. In the churches, with the glint of candles replacing the glint of flowing water, the mosaics leaped from the walls.

The earliest surviving Christian mosaics date from about A.D. 395, when the Emperor Theodosius I converted the great domed mausoleum of the pagan Emperor Galerius at Salonika into a church. Some of these mosaics, including the Pantocrator on the dome, have been shattered by earthquakes, but the martyred saints standing in prayer along the frieze of the dome have survived to demonstrate that the earliest makers of Christian mosaics had already achieved a superb mastery of the material. There is nothing in the least hesitant about the design. The saints in their brown, purple, and shimmering white vestments stand with uplifted arms before the airy palaces and citadels of heaven. In a fantastic perspective we see the golden city, an immense palace ringing the dome, with its solemn archways and arcades leading to the unknown splendors within. No doubt the heavenly mansions were designed after the earthly mansions of the emperors, with their sumptuous elegance and jeweled adornments; and the saints themselves with their refined features and casual grace may have been modeled after the princes and officials of the Christian court. Yet the effect is one of overwhelming beauty, and this ring of saints is made completely credible. Peacocks stand on the walls of the heavenly city, and this too becomes credible as you gaze at that incredible dome.

Earthquakes have left cracks and fissures like tongues of flame eating into the heavenly city, but the general effect is one of sustained magnificence. Few visitors come to this vast domed church, and one can stand for hours beneath the saints and the golden palaces with no other companions than the swallows who build their nests in the eaves. In the history of Christian art this ancient mausoleum, now known as the church or the rotunda of Saint George, holds a special place. Here, so far as is known, are the first Christian mosaics, executed with a refinement never to be excelled.

There are other astonishing things in the rotunda of Saint George, including a barrel vault which is encrusted with mosaics of birds, apples, pomegranates, and pears, all set against the midnight blue of space, hovering in a strange detachment, as though a curtain had been let down to reveal all that was rich and beautiful and succulent. The barrel vault is remarkably deficient in Christian symbolism, for these birds and fruit suggest a very earthly feast. Not far from the church there stands the triumphal arch of Galerius, while closer at hand there is the minaret which once summoned the Turks to prayer, the lone survivor of the hundreds of minarets which once crowded the city of Salonika.

Today Salonika has the largest collection of mosaics in the world. Nowhere else are there so many mosaics from so many periods by masters working within the imperial tradition. High up above the port, in a district now cluttered with workmen's dwellings, there can be found the small monastic church of Hosios David, so small a church that it could easily be contained in an ordinary living room. In the apse Christ in glory appears to Ezekiel and Habakkuk in a composition which can be dated to the middle years of the fifth century. Christ wears a blue gown laced with reddish-gold threads. He sits enthroned on a rainbow, guarded by angels, a bull, and a lion. The holy rivers of Paradise flow at his feet, and the *mandorla* takes the form of a great luminous sail billowing in the winds of heaven. Habakkuk sits on the right, deep in contemplation, gazing at a book on his knees, while Ezekiel, seeing the vision before his eyes, throws up his hands in a gesture of surprise and wonder. But what is chiefly remarkable about the mosaic is the delicacy and beauty of the central figure, the Christ in his blue robes, with a blue hood, beardless and feminine, so that at first glance he appears to be a woman, and for a moment one imagines it is the Virgin riding the rainbow. This is not the Pantocrator but a dreaming youth of grave beauty, following an ancient tradition by which Christ was represented in the fullness of his youth and lost in his dreams. Never again, so far as we know, was he to be represented in this way, so grave, so beautiful, so calm in the assumption of authority. He gazes straight out of the apse, oblivious of the presence of Habakkuk bent over his book or the wildly excited Ezekiel. Power does not stream from him; he wears his authority with ease and with a quiet splendor.

There are few portraits of Christ so enchanting as this. In that small church he is on the same level as the worshiper, not towering, not dominating, no larger than the people who come to pay him homage. The mosaic, which was covered with plaster by the Turks, remained hidden for centuries, being uncovered only in 1921, not long after Salonika became a Greek city for the first time since the Turkish conquest.

At the more famous Basilica of Saint Demetrius in Salonika, built according to tradition on the site of the synagogue where Saint Paul preached, time has played a strange game with the mosaics, for while some have perished during the fires, others long hidden have come to light. There must have been a time when the entire basilica was covered with mosaics, but today there are only a few surviving panels embedded on the columns and on the piers of the sanctuary, the best of them dating from the seventh century. The church was burned down in 1917, and the surviving mosaics must be regarded as miraculously preserved relics from a remote past.

Saint Demetrius was martyred during the persecutions of Diocletian and Galerius in A.D. 303. Twenty years later Constantine became sole emperor, and about this time the saint's body was discovered; it was said to have exuded a wonderful and perpetual perfume. On the site of his martyrdom a small church was built, and the saint's body was placed reverently in the crypt.

Saint Demetrius had been a soldier, but he was remembered as a sweet-tempered and handsome youth with a narrow face and a pointed chin. So he appears, always recognizably the same, in the mosaics. Usually he wears a shimmering gown adorned with the *tablion,* the square of colored cloth which serves to indicate a high rank in the Byzantine court, and he throws his arms over the shoulders of the children or bishops who are under his protection. The young face set in the golden halo has a hallucinatory quality, and it is not difficult to believe that it is a faithful rendering of the patron saint of Salonika. There is an air of naturalness about the saint, and no one would be particularly surprised if he stepped out of the mosaics, for he resembles many of the fine-boned Greek youths one sees today.

But in the great church of Hagia Sophia in Salonika that air of casual naturalness is lacking. No martyrs were buried there, to bring the sweetness of humanity and the perfume of their bodies into the presence of the worshipers. When the emperor was in residence in Salonika, this was the court church dedicated to Christ, recognized at the Council of Nicaea, the first ecumenical council, as Hagia Sophia, the Holy Wisdom. On the vast dome a strangely contorted Christ was represented on a rainbow, while the apostles gazed from below, twisting their heads to see him more clearly. While this twisting of the heads must be accounted among the most brilliant inventions of the mosaicists' art, because it gives to the apostles an appearance remote from ordinary humanity, so that they resemble strange spiritual fruit rather than men, nevertheless the distortion involves an element of strain. Not all the apostles gaze upward. A few are sunk in meditation, and some seem to be reeling at the thought of the Saviour ascending to heaven and vanishing from their sight. The portraits of Saint Demetrius are merely icons. On the dome of Hagia Sophia is a dramatic representation of the Ascension, a scene of vast and tumultuous power. Only the Virgin, praying beneath the rainbow-colored clouds, remains calm in the knowledge that Christ is merely returning to his familiar home.

Of the other, and far more famous, Hagia Sophia at Constantinople, it has always been difficult to speak, for words fail to conjure up the sheer immensity and daring of its construction. When Justinian in the incredible space of six years built the cathedral on the ruins of a church destroyed by rioting fanatics, he exclaimed: "Glory to God who hath counted me to perform so great a work. Solomon, I have surpassed thee!" It was an understandable boast. Justinian went on to command that the walls should represent the fields of Paradise and the star-studded dome should represent the infinite spaces of heaven.

Most, and perhaps all, of the mosaics created in his time have vanished. Once the whole vast unbelievable building shone with mosaics; now there are only a few patches here and there, consisting of portraits of later emperors and empresses offering their gifts to Christ. High up in a semidome a Virgin smiles, and when the light catches her, her radiance can fill the church. But it is the *Deesis* in the south gallery which is generally admitted to be the most masterly mosaic composition in the entire history of the art. We see Saint John the Baptist and the Virgin standing in entreaty before Christ, interceding for all the sinners of the world. Only the head and shoulders of the Virgin remain, and the heads and busts of Christ and the Baptist. Christ is serene majesty, calm amid the storms, youthful through bearded, only hinting at His power. He is kingly, as the Virgin is queenly, inclining her head in an attitude of grave sweetness. Christ wears a gold tunic and a blue gown; one hand is raised in blessing, the other grasps the gold-bound Gospels. But it is in the figure of Saint John the Baptist that the Byzantine master has demonstrated his superlative sense of the tragedy of intercession, the head bent, the face lined with care, the half-closed eyes filled with yearning and protestation. The bronze-colored hair sweeps backward in waves of power; the darker beard is tangled with despair. With extraordinary intensity and realism the artist has depicted a tragically beautiful and very human face confronted with the impassive majesty of divinity. He is the precursor, the *prodromos*, but he is also, as the artist has depicted him, the one who intercedes most powerfully on behalf of the sinners of this world.

The *Deesis* panel, originally eighteen feet high, was uncovered by Dr. Thomas Whittemore in 1933. No one knows for certain when it was created, and various dates between 1150 and 1270 have been suggested. There are no inscriptions which would indicate a more precise date. All that is certain is that the unknown artist was among the greatest who ever lived.

This panel was made at a time when the tradition was already dying and demonstrates the amazing power of the mosaicist to bring new life to a dying art. Indeed, in the twelfth and thirteenth centuries the Byzantine artists brought about an extraordinary renaissance of feeling. Once again, as in the fifth century, they were able to paint the walls with freshness and delight in colored stones. The calm two-dimensional figures of earlier centuries gave way to more subtle three-dimensional figures. This Christ lives and breathes, and in a moment the Baptist will fall to his knees, hot tears springing from his half-closed eyes.

The *Deesis* is almost lost in the immensity of Hagia Sophia, and we can no longer imagine the appearance of the church when it was covered with many masterpieces. Hagia Sophia was consecrated to "Christ the Holy Wisdom," but there is a sense in which it was consecrated to Christ, "Light of Light," as He is described in the Nicene

Creed. This house was the abode of light, for the Greeks never doubted that light was holy. For them light was the sap of life, a power driving through nature, palpable and beautiful, and therefore possessing the likeness of Christ. In that seething world of fluid colors, the walls having no more substance than flame, all the corners rounded by mosaics, the Byzantines found their earthly peace and their promise of peace in heaven. Out of this adoration of light they created their pure and enduring art.

Plates

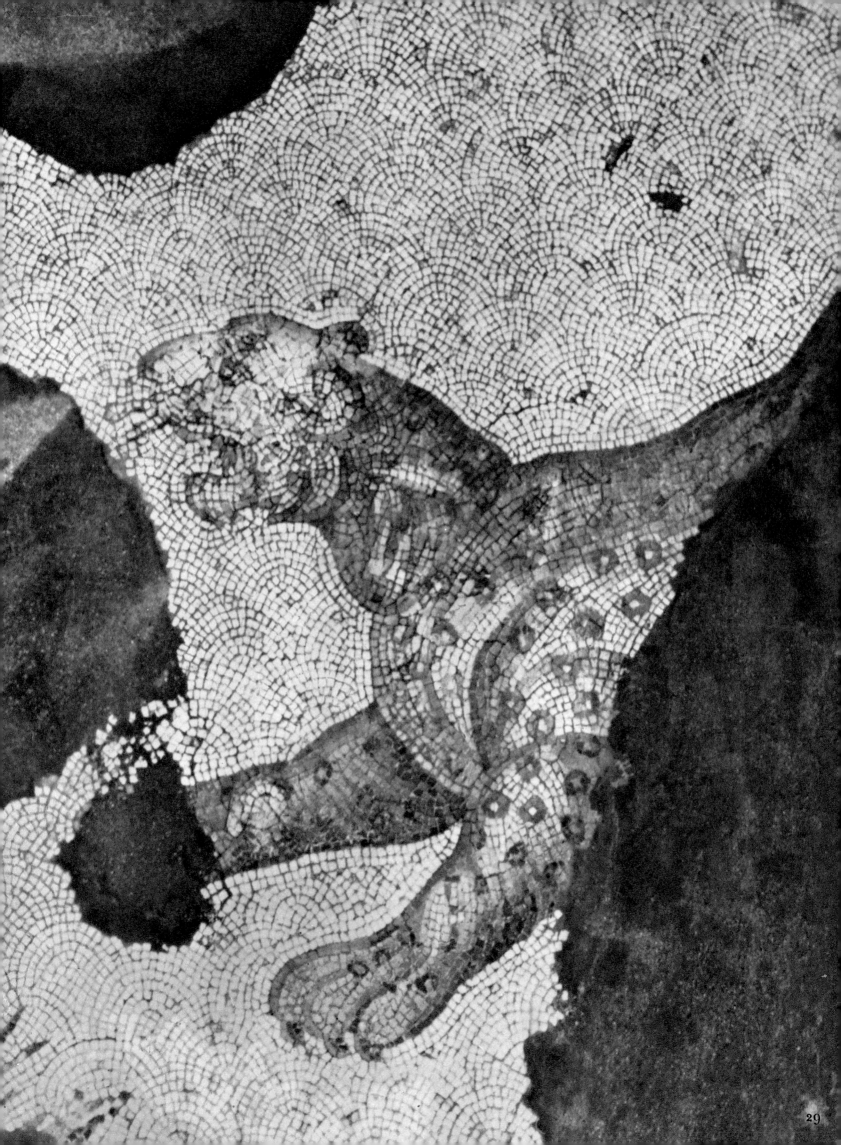

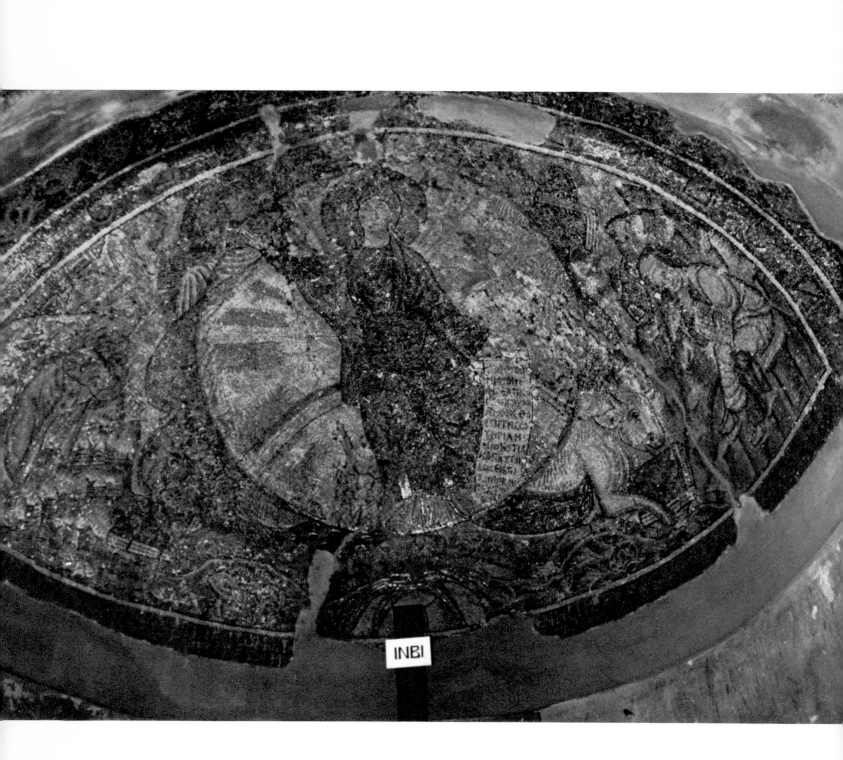

Ο ΑΡ ΟΜΕΓΑC   ΜΙΧΑ ΓΗΛ ΑΧΗ

48

An aged man is but a paltry thing,
A tattered coat upon a stick, unless
Soul clap its hands and sing, and louder sing
For every tatter in its mortal dress,
Nor is there singing school but studying
Monuments of its own magnificence;
And therefore I have sailed the seas and come
To the holy city of Byzantium.

The poet who wrote these lines never saw Byzantium in the flesh, and never traveled through the Byzantine empire except in the spirit. His learning came from books and mythologies, and the impulse for the poem seems to have sprung from a chance encounter with the words of a chronicler who described a tree made of gold and silver with artificial birds singing in it which was once to be found in the Emperor's palace in Byzantium. The poem "Sailing to Byzantium," which appears to have been written in a single breath, occupied his attention for many months; and as he celebrated that superb artificiality which is the greatest art, he was himself practicing an art riddled with artifices. For him Byzantium was the heaven of the artist, the supreme embodiment of all the greatest achievements of artistic skill. Byzantium was the mysterious land where the artist finds himself at last, as Jerusalem was the mysterious land where the saints find themselves with their dying breaths.

Yeats had no need to sail across the Sea of Marmara to reach his holy land, for it was a place he had often visited in his dreams. In his fancy the golden birds took wing, and the tree flowered; in the palace of the Emperor only the superb artificers were honored. It was only later that the poet began to study the history of Byzantium, the earthly city, finding in it a reflection of the heavenly city he had imagined.

"I think that in early Byzantium," he wrote in *A Vision* (New York: Macmillan, 1956), "maybe never before or since in recorded history, religious, aesthetic and practical life were one, that architects and artificers . . . spoke to the multitude and the few alike." It is a breathtaking claim, and very largely true; the inhabitants of Christian Byzantium would have taken it in their stride. They may have half despised their emperors and mistrusted their priests, but the glory of the city was a perpetual reminder of their common brotherhood, and there was a special glory attached to their churches, which were more than places of worship. Within the walls of the church many of the functions of the ancient Greek *agora* were preserved. Here political feuds began; here gossip was artfully circulated and assignations were made. Battles were fought in the churches, not doctrinal battles only. The church was so beautiful that it seemed to offer a foretaste of Paradise, and it was the haunt of scheming men, chattering women, and wild-eyed children who romped among the columns.

Life flowed through the Byzantine churches on all the days of the week, not only on Sundays and saints' days. The ritual pageantry of the church was equaled only by the pageantry of daily life. At night the churches came into their own; for while the night offices were celebrated there was a blaze of fire from silver lamps, glowing lanterns, candelabras, and massed candles. Then the hammered gold of the altar and the *iconostasis*, and all the glinting mosaics, spread their diffuse and other-worldly light across the whole length of the church, so that the entire building seemed to be on fire. "Luminous night,' says the Byzantine poet, "took on the hues of the rose," but it was a rose of many colors, the petals waving in the winds of heaven.

Those ceremonies often lasted all night, as they still do in the monasteries of Mount Athos. The chanting continues until at last toward dawn it seems to rise and fall with the pulse of the heartbeats, coming not from the choristers but from one's own body and soul. The night-long drama presented in the church seems to be taking place within oneself: the temple becomes the worshiper. Above all there was the sense of a splendor beyond human comprehension, of a mystery which became more mysterious the more one penetrated into its heart. How great the splendor was we know from the Russian chronicler who accompanied Vladimir, Grand Prince of Kiev, to Constantinople about A.D. 989. He describes how the Grand Prince visited many countries in search of a faith, and found them all wanting—"there was no glory in them"—until he reached Greece:

> Then we went on to Greece, and the Greeks led us to the edifices where they worship their God, and we knew not whether we were in heaven or on earth. For on earth there is no such splendor or such beauty, and we are at a loss how to describe it. We know only that God dwells there among men, and the service is fairer than the ceremonies of other nations. For we cannot forget that beauty.

Sometimes the barbarians who visited the court of the Byzantine emperors and attended their churches reported that they had beheld angels falling from heaven in order to mingle with the priests and officiate at the ceremonies.

Every device was being employed by the inventive Byzantines to create the atmosphere of worship and belief. The priests in their rainbow-colored robes, the silver organs accompanying the choirs, the swinging of censers, the intricacy of the ceremonies, the moments of high drama, and the long surging intervals when there was no drama at all, all these were conceived as separate parts of a service which remained one and indivisible although it was in fact an astonishing amalgam of many widely different themes. To a quite extraordinary extent Byzantine worship was contrived, but it was none the less deeply religious for being artificial. "We cannot forget that beauty," wrote the Russian chronicler, and it was precisely in order that the beauty should be unforgettable that the services took on a deliberately contrived character.

Among all these contrivances the artists, as always, played their special role. The walls of mosaics, which seem not to have been made by human hands, were the work of trained craftsmen belonging to craft guilds with their own secret laws and their carefully guarded privileges. They were under imperial supervision and control, entry into the guilds being closely watched by examiners appointed by the state. There was a system of apprenticeship and a graduated scale of payment. According to an edict published in the reign of Diocletian, the chief designer of the mosaics, known as the *pictor imaginarius,* received one hundred and seventy-five sesterces, while a draftsman, known as the *pictor parietarius,* received seventy-five sesterces; the workmen—the men who cut and chipped the stones, and those who embedded them in the plaster—received between fifty and sixty sesterces. This was daily pay and compared favorably with the rates of pay at the time. No precise figures are available for the payments made to the mosaicists in Byzantine times, but we may assume that they were roughly in the same proportion.

The *pictor imaginarius* was the kingpin around which all the others revolved. He worked hand in hand with the architect of the church and was far more than a designer. He painted the scenes on models, prepared the cartoons, supervised the draftsmen and the laborers, and provided the creative force. A whole church or a whole wall would be entrusted to him, with the result that the free flow of a single man's imagination can be observed working over large areas. A small church might be the work of a single mosaic master, while a large church might be divided among seven or eight masters with a supreme designer in charge of the whole. The draftsmen were merely the tools of the *pictores imaginarii.* Some would concentrate on heads, others on gowns, and still others on ornamental borders, on rocks, and on the gold backgrounds. No doubt only the very best workmen were entrusted with the work on the faces, for it was in the portrayal of emotion in the human face that the success or failure of the mosaic depended. An extreme division of labor was practiced, and we may imagine that the master, like Rubens supervising his army of assistants, put in the finishing touches which brought the entire design into focus.

Indeed, the making of mosaics was like painting, and intimately related to the art of painting, with the difference that many different arts went into the compositions. It was not enough to know how to apply color to a wall. The *pictor imaginarius* must know the art of gem-cutting, the refractive powers of precious and semiprecious stones, the properties of glass fused with gold and silver leaf, the subtle effects brought about by setting dominant and recessive colors side by side. The mosaic masters learned very early that an effect of increased depth and luminosity was acquired by painting the plaster red just before the stones were inserted, with the result that where the *tessellae* have fallen away we sometimes see a patch of rust color which was once bright cinnabar. The mosaic masters had to learn the difficult art of outlining the figures delicately and sharply against the surrounding gold, which always threatened to drown out the figures. He had to learn, too, as the Impressionists learned more than a thousand years later, to resolve his colors out of many different shades, so that an eyelid might be painted green and yellow, a nostril blue and cherry red, or a mouth might be outlined in gold and pink, or a cheek shadowed in vermilion and ochre, to produce an effect of naturalness. It was a *pointilliste* art, and with mosaics, therefore, unlike most paintings, there was always a precise point of focus where they could be seen to best advantage, and this point for the wall mosaics was usually about eight feet away from the wall at an angle of forty-five degrees. Very rarely were mosaics brought down to the level of the church floor. They were to be looked at from below, so that they appeared to hover overhead in the changing light of the candles.

The mosaic masters were painters in light and stone, practicing an art which was sometimes closer to sculpture than to painting. It was a strange art, for the prodigious effects were related to the reverberations of light in the church, which were scarcely susceptible to analysis, for although the fragments of the mosaic were hard and motionless, the light was fluid, changing direction with every passing shadow, and with every new candle flame.

Every master developed his own style, which was subordinated to the general style of the church. None of the mosaics are signed, and we can rarely date them with accuracy, with the result that reputable scholars have differed by as much as three hundred years in dating a mosaic. In time, when we have come to know them better, they will be given names like the names we give to the painters of Attic pottery and the makers of medieval woodcuts. We shall speak of the Master of the *Deesis* at Hagia Sophia or the Master of the Baptism at Daphni. Since a complete corpus of Byzantine mosaics has never been put together, and the study of the various styles is still in its infancy, there are large areas of the art which remain unexplored.

In this elaborate and ceremonial art cultivated by a small elite of master craftsmen in the capital of the empire, we may expect to find the greatest compositions in the private chapels of the emperor and the empress, and in those vast and magnificently adorned chambers where the imperial family lived and worshiped and granted audiences. In these chambers the secular and the religious met on equal terms, for we hear of the imperial bedchamber studded with mosaics from floor to ceiling, the floor shining with the peacock, the symbol of eternal life and power, the arched ceiling bright with stars, and each wall resplendent with a golden cross. Along the lower part of the wall there was a border of spring flowers. On the walls of other chambers there would be portraits of the imperial family, or renderings of the emperor's triumphant campaigns, or the visitor would be confronted with the inevitable scene of the emperor or the empress standing before Christ, who offers them the crown of the empire. Unhappily, the Byzantine palaces in Constantinople have all been destroyed, and there remain as far as we know—for much more remains to be discovered—only the fragments of a mosaic pavement dating from the reign of Justinian. It is an interesting pavement, but no one has been able to make any sense out of it. We see a girl carrying a waterpot, a boy feeding a reluctant donkey, a man leading his two sons on a camel, an eagle in the coils of a serpent, a bare-kneed warrior in combat with a tiger. These scenes are thrown down on the pavement with no apparent order, and it has been suggested that it was simply the decoration for the play-yard of the imperial children. The Master of the Imperial Play-yard has a recognizable style, and if another mosaic made by him were discovered, we would recognize it instantly.

In the mosaics the style is everything, and we can recognize with no great effort the hand of the master as distinguished from that of the bungling restorer. We recognize a certain palette, a certain grouping of figures, a certain curving line which may be repeated endlessly. So we find in the small monastery church at Daphni six miles west of Athens on the highroad to Eleusis a single recognizable master who designed and worked on the panels describing the life of Christ, while another worked on the cycle of the Virgin, a third on the saints and angels, and a fourth—the most daring and imaginative of all—was responsible for the great Pantocrator on the dome. These four masters produced mosaics of such beauty that Daphni must be accounted among the supreme masterpieces of Byzantine art.

The visitor coming down the dusty road and seeing the high walls of the monastery and the cypresses around the low-domed church is scarcely prepared for the splendors within. It looks like one of many hundreds of Byzantine churches with no particular nobility of design. There is a coffee shop across the street, heavy trucks thunder down the road, which follows the line of the ancient sacred way of the pilgrims to the Eleusinian mysteries, and soon, no doubt, Daphni will become another factory town like all the other factory towns of suburban Athens. A small path leads through poppies and knee-high grasses to the monastery gates, and even when you are in the courtyard with its Norman arcade and the remnants of columns which belonged to the ancient temple of Apollo Daphnephorus, the bearer of laurels, there is no indication that this is a specially hallowed place. For at least twenty-five hundred years there has been a temple here. At first it was dedicated to Apollo, the youthful god of the winged intelligence, and then the goddess Demeter and her daughter Persephone and Athena came to dwell with him, and when later it became a Christian church the memory of the laurels sacred to Apollo remained, for it was dedicated to the holy *Chrysodaphniotissa,* the Virgin of the Golden Laurels.

The Christian church has had a strange history. Founded in the fifth century, it fell into a decline during the barbarian invasions of the ninth century. The French barons who later ruled over Athens seized and partially rebuilt the church in A.D. 1205, and until the fourteenth century it remained in the possession of the Cistercian monks. Then it became the private chapel of a powerful Florentine banking family, the Acciajuoli. Here Franco Acciajuoli, the last claimant to the Duchy of Athens, was garroted by order of the Pasha of Thessaly when all this region came under Turkish dominion. The Turks converted the church into a mosque, and so it remained until the Greek War of Independence, although there were brief intervals when the Turks magnanimously granted the monks the right to worship there. At various times in the nineteenth century it was a powder magazine, a police station, a lunatic asylum, and a sheep pen.

The wonder is that so many of the mosaics survived. There are whole stretches of wall where all the mosaics have vanished. Two sling-bolts of Frankish manufacture were found embedded in the figure of the great Pantocrator on the dome, and it is assumed that the Turks amused themselves by firing at the portrait of the Christian God before covering it with plaster. The plaster protected it for four hundred years, but there was no way of protecting the lower walls from the incursions of Turkish soldiers, Greek policemen, lunatics, and sheep.

The church in its present form was probably built by the Emperor Basil II, under whom the empire reached the summit of its power and glory. A date about A.D. 1020 has been suggested, and cannot be far wrong. The mosaics are the work of craftsmen from the Byzantine court, men trained in the imperial tradition. One *pictor imaginarius* achieved a supreme masterpiece: that portrait of God the Father, all energy and wrath, which fills the dome and seems to fill the universe. There at last the Byzantine artist painted the unpaintable.

That portrait of God derives across the centuries from Olympian Zeus, and more precisely from the chryselephantine statue of Zeus created by Phidias for the temple at Olympia. But where Phidias depicted the august monarch of heaven, serene and imperturbable, the Christian mosaicist depicted a spiritual being of unimaginable power, monarch of all universes, the judge of the quick and the dead. He is the God who says, "Be still, and know that I am God."

It is an astonishing portrait, and the more one looks at it the more astonishing it becomes. Only six colors—white, black, brown, red, blue, and gold—have gone into the making of that portrait. The heavy, deeply lined face is set on a massive neck, the shoulders are draped in a brilliant blue gown, and one gnarled hand clutches the golden binding of the Gospels. The face is white, framed in thick hair and a dark and ominous beard; it is almost a sketch done in charcoal. Set in a rainbow colored circle, with a cross formed of blue stones in a golden halo, the face has a rawness and a grandeur unequaled in Byzantine art. The firmament has been rolled back and we see the face of the living God.

Here at last is God in his starkness and plainness, in his terror and beauty, in his solicitude for all created things. This majestic portrait of the *Rex tremendae majestatis* seems to have captured that element which cannot be captured—the superhuman power, the energy of God. With a shock one realizes later that the face of God is only a little more than five feet long.

In the superb panel of the Baptism of Christ we see John the Baptist with long hair and wild beard reaching across the river Jordan to touch the head of Christ, who stands in the trembling waters in the familiar posture of an ancient Greek *kouros*. Here again the Hellenic influence can be felt, and indeed all the mosaics at Daphni are deeply influenced by classic Greek art. Christ stands in the water in unworldly glory and transcendental beauty, not yet of this world, surprised and a little fearful of the blessedness which has been granted to him, rejoicing in the presence of the dove and the angels. Though half of the mosaic has been ruined by time, what survives has the perfection which re-creates the whole.

In the Nativity again we meet the calm Hellenic element in the robust curly-headed angels who gaze upon the Christ child in His manger. Here the black cave-mouth has the effect of making the Child stand out in relief, and once again, as in the Pantocrator, the essential elements are outlined in stark black and white. The swaddling bands, the angels' gowns, the manger are white, and the darkness of the cave-mouth subtly continues the dark blue of the Virgin's gown, that gown which is like a protective wave lapping at the shore of the manger. As in nearly all the Byzantine mosaics of the Nativity, the Virgin is seen lying beside the manger, only her head raised a little above the level of the ground. In the austerity of the Virgin there is a classic dignity. She is not the half-sleeping, exhausted Mother to be found on many icons, but fully awake, fiercely protective, with something about her of Pallas Athena.

In the lonely monastic church of Hosios Lukas high up in the hills of Phocis, not far from the crossroads where Oedipus killed his father, the mosaics shine in even greater splendor. There seems never to have been a time when they were covered with plaster; it was too far away, too unimportant to attract the attention of the Turks, with the result that of all the surviving churches with mosaics, this is the one which preserves most faithfully the original designs. Here and there, as in the magnificent Virgin in the apse and the triumphant Pentecost in the dome, we are aware of court artists working within a tradition of deliberate refinement, but the total effect is one of brilliant chaos. The classic calm gives way to romantic excitement. Every column has its medallion portraits of saints, so many of them that they are beyond counting; every cranny, every corner must be filled with the testimony of sanctity, and the eye has nowhere to rest. Hosios Lukas—the church was dedicated not to Saint Luke the Evangelist but to a local saint, the hermit Loukas the Stiriot, who died in A.D. 946—has the pleasant garishness of a child's highly colored toy.

So at Hosios Lukas, instead of the calm Athena-like Madonna guarding her child, we see her full of anxiety, her hands hovering over the child's head, aware of the dangers that threaten him, those dangers which are symbolically represented by the crossed swaddling bands. There is strain and uneasiness, the knowledge of storms to come, violence in the air. In this church no one is at rest: the saints clamor to be heard. The best of the mosaics show huddled groups of men, fishermen or soldiers, going about their mysterious work, whispering urgently to one another. Saint Lukas can be seen flinging up his hands in an act of benediction which is like an act of protest, his dark pointed beard, his headdress, his elbows, and his gown all forming insistent triangles. Compare the dark and saturnine Lukas with the youthful Demetrius at Salonika, and you recognize at once that this is a monastic church where only the monks gathered. An intense monkish excitement pervades Hosios Lukas; the gold of the columns clashes against the gold of the walls, and there is restlessness everywhere.

Perhaps it was inevitable that there should be an absence of composure in a large monastic community set down in the remote hills far from the towns. In the much smaller monastery at Kaisariani, close to Athens on the slopes of Mount Hymettus, among the pines and the centuries-old cypresses, on a site once sacred to the goddess Aphrodite because a holy spring, possessing the power to relieve women of the pains of childbirth, came out of the ground, another aspect of Byzantine art is presented. The small monastery church at Kaisariani makes no pretensions to grandeur. The blue mountain, all barren and clean as a bone, stretches into the distance, and the church lies at the foot of the mountain in a patch of greenness. The stream murmurs, the trees sough in the wind. Dwarfed by the trees, the red-roofed church lies close to the earth, scarcely larger than a forester's hut; and men come here to enjoy the shade, to listen to the stream, and to smell the pines, while the women come, as they have come for centuries, to drink the holy waters. In the church the sixteenth-century frescoes are flaking away. They are good frescoes, based on the famous designs of Panselinos, but they make no demands on the beholder; they are like the familiar illustrations of a book one knows by heart.

In Kaisariani the great imperial tradition at last falls away. It is not only that magnificence would be out of place in this setting, but it would be irrelevant to build magnificently here. In this quiet valley there is no need for panoply, for what is being celebrated is ultimately beyond the reach of the artist. What is being celebrated is not the grandeur and power of Christ, but His patience and humility, His quietness and repose.

Plates

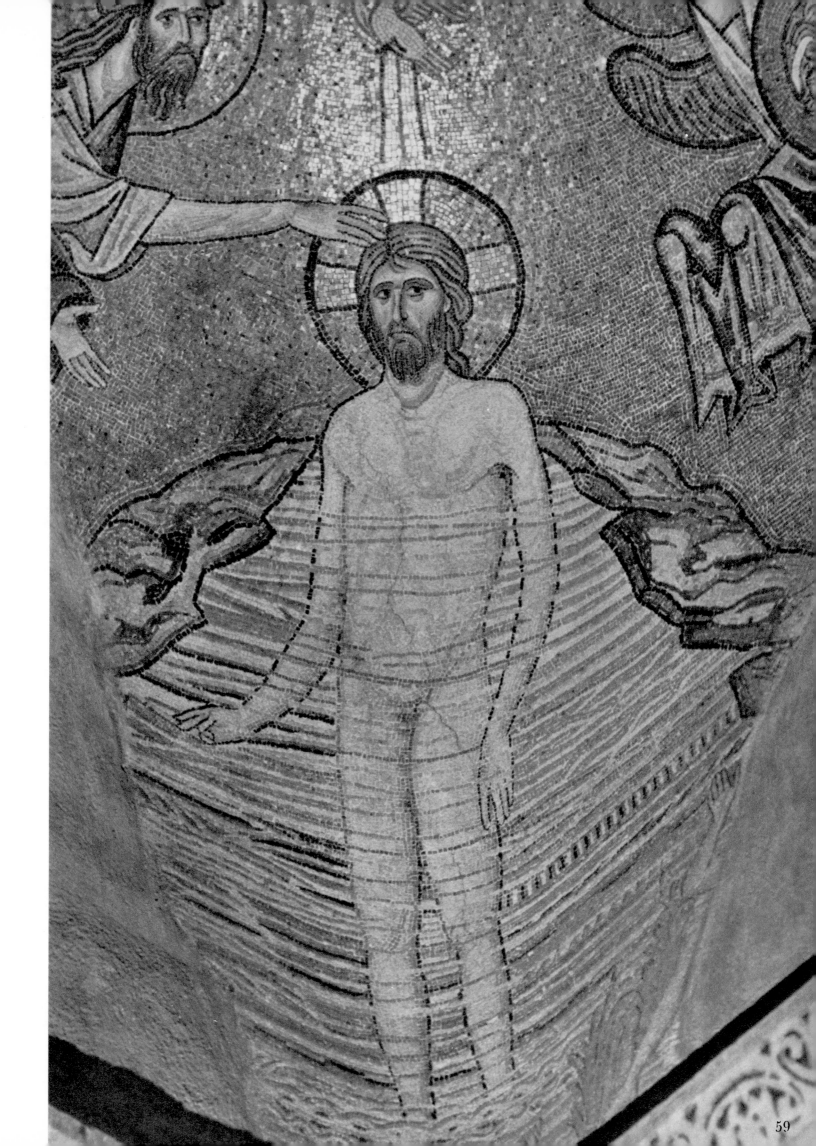

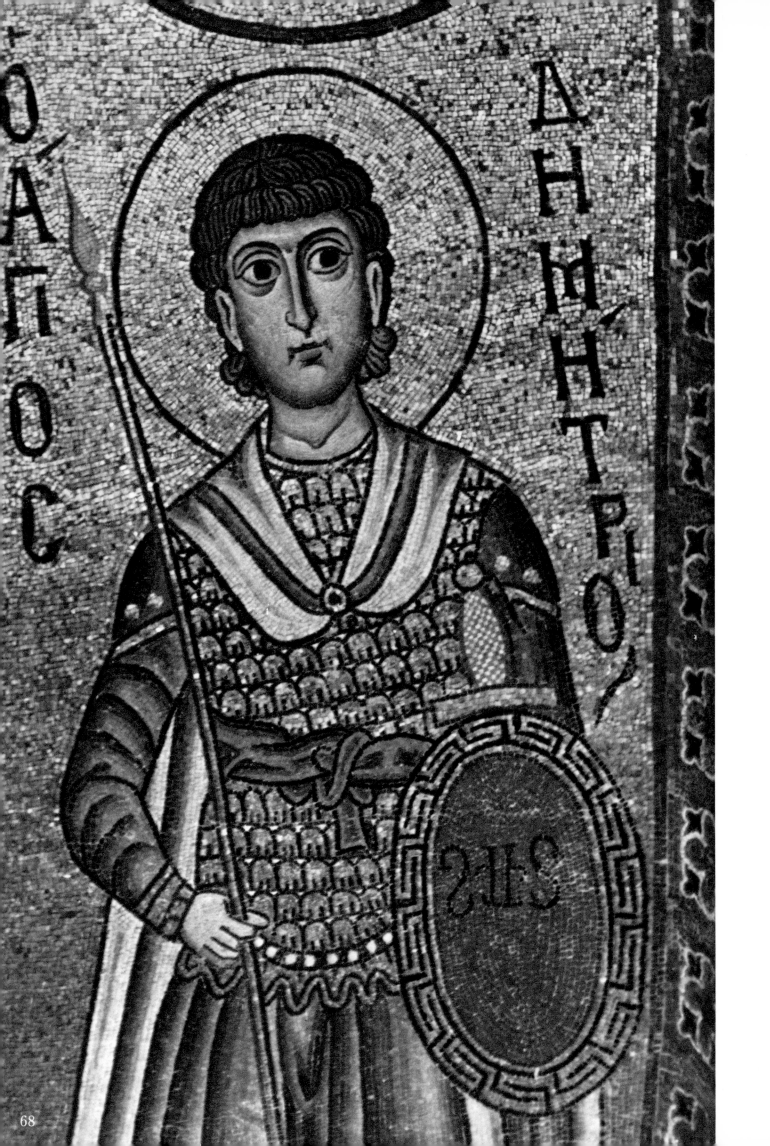

ΟΝΙΠΤΗΡ

74

75

Ο ΑΓΙΟΣ ΠΑΥΛΟΣ

Once out of nature I shall never take
My bodily form from any natural thing,
But such a form as Grecian goldsmiths make
Of hammered gold and gold enamelling
To keep a drowsy emperor awake;
Or set upon a golden bough to sing
To lords and ladies of Byzantium
Of what is past, or passing, or to come.

So one returns again and again to that strangely evocative poem which seems to contain within it so many secrets of Byzantium, as though the art of a thousand years were being crystallized in a single poem. Yeats's notebooks have survived, and we can see him working patiently toward this final statement of his poetic beliefs, catching them on the wing before the idea is fully expressed and the full measure of the vision is granted to him. For him Byzantium is a glory, a splendor beyond all imagining, and because he is a poet, he must compel himself to imagine it.

There is nothing tentative in the early drafts of the poem. There is much scratching and interpolating; ideas arise and die away, to be replaced by others as the focus recedes or advances into the foreground; but the central theme is stated in the first words he wrote in his notebook. According to his habit he began to think out the poem in prose. He wrote: "I therefore travel towards Byzantium. . . . I fly from things becoming to the thing become. . . . I fly from nature to Byzantium. . . ." There he seems to have left the thought for some days, to ponder its outcome with the assurance that he was already close to the heart of the mystery. The journey is conceived as a flight, and when later he gave the poem a title, calling it "Sailing to Byzantium," he meant by "sailing" far more than a journey in a ship; for he was speaking of a flight of the soul into the unknown regions where art achieves its ultimate perfection and its ultimate justification.

From the beginning it becomes clear that Byzantium is more than the great city on the Golden Horn, although it contains the city. Byzantium is the City of God, the ultimate abode of the artist, the place of visions. The golden bird, the drowsy emperor, the goldsmiths at their work are symbols for presences far more enduring than birds, emperors, or workmen: they represent a world beyond nature, remote from the living and breathing flesh, existing in another universe altogether. What appears as an artificial bird on an artificial tree becomes the human soul in its headlong flight to create eternal art. The soul flies "from things becoming to the thing become." It leaps out of nature altogether to enter the world of ideas and to lose itself in them. Driven by a rage for perfection, it creates an art which is perfect because it no longer appears to be made by human hands but on the contrary appears to have been made by some divinity to please "a drowsy emperor," who is himself divine, being God or the possessor of God-like attributes, the superb divinity who rules over the realm of art, the kingdom of all perfect things.

Perhaps "the lords and ladies of Byzantium" are the saints and angels surrounding the throne of the drowsy emperor—drowsy because he is old as the universe, or all the universes, but also perhaps because he is in a trancelike state, or perhaps because he is happily satiated with those supreme works of art which are offered to him like prayers.

In this way Yeats reaches out to encompass the unknown world of Byzantium, which is dimly present in the historical Byzantium with its myriad domes, its golden birds, and brilliant illuminations. It was precisely this world which was created by the Byzantine masters of mosaic. It was a world so remote that it could not be reached, so unthinkable that it could not be imagined. Nevertheless they reached it and imagined it.

The triumph of Yeats was that he could penetrate so accurately, and with an appearance of ease, into the imagination of the Byzantines. He had read Porphyry and Plotinus, but always in English translation and in quick snatches. He was no scholar, and would not have been able to distinguish one Byzantine emperor from another. Out of a remembered phrase from Plotinus—"The soul flies from things becoming to the thing become"—and the image of a bird made of hammered gold, he created the image of a civilization and of an ideal world in which all that is past, passing, and to come is gathered together.

For the Byzantine masters the world of the imagination was very much as Yeats imagined it. It was a world where the temporal had vanished entirely, and all the accidents of change were forgotten in the contemplation of the unchanging splendors of eternity. There was no sensual music, no bearing and begetting, no heartache, no joy, no sorrow. It was a world of blessedness, "the thing become," beyond all becoming and all knowing. In this world there was a golden bird in full-throated song.

In 1907, twenty years before Yeats wrote "Sailing to Byzantium," he visited Ravenna in the company of Lady Gregory. It was a very brief visit—they hurried through Florence, Milan, Urbino, Ferrara, and Ravenna in a few days—and the journey left little impression on his poetry, which was still preoccupied with the myths of Ireland, with falling rhythms, and with dreamlike images. In Ravenna he saw his first mosaics, and the full splendor of Byzantine art was opened out to him.

Like Constantinople and Salonika, Ravenna was an imperial city. For the better part of the fifth century it was the capital of the Western Roman Emperor, and there, about A.D. 440, the Empress Galla Placidia erected for herself and her family the cruciform mausoleum which is today her chief claim to our affection. In her own day she was known for her beauty, her diplomacy, and the splendor of the buildings she erected during her long reign, and especially she was known for the strange fortune which made her successively a Roman princess, Queen of the Goths, and Roman Empress. She was the daughter of the Emperor Theodosius, and when the Goths attacked Rome they carried her off in triumph as one more of the trophies to decorate the victories of Alaric, King of the Goths. At Narbonne she married Ataulfus, Alaric's youthful successor, in a sumptuous ceremony attended by the former Roman Emperor Attalus, now reduced to the status of a choir leader, for he led the wedding song. Ataulfus, abandoning Italy and Gaul, set up his new capital in Barcelona, and when he was murdered by an unruly groom, Galla Placidia was permitted to return to Rome, where her half-brother Honorius was emperor, in exchange for a ransom of half a million measures of wheat. Honorius insisted that she marry his co-emperor, Constantius, but she was in love with the memory of Ataulfus and delayed the marriage to that loose-limbed, bullet-headed soldier with the glaring eyes as long as possible. Constantius was more savage than the barbarian Goths; he was a wild tippler, and liked to amuse himself by joining the buffoons when they entertained at court. After the death of Honorius, he reigned for seven months and then died, leaving the empire to Galla Placidia as regent for his young children. The children grew up into weaklings; the Empress was strong. For a quarter of a century she ruled the Western Empire from her capital in Ravenna.

Once, when she was saved from shipwreck, she built the great Basilica of Saint John the Evangelist, who had listened to her prayers and miraculously saved her life. The mosaics on the walls of the basilica recounted all the stages of that divine intervention, and it was remembered that even the pavings of the basilica represented waves. Her portrait and the portraits of all the members of her family decorated the basilica, which was clearly erected in her own honor. The basilica has long since vanished, but the mausoleum remains. It was designed during the last years of her reign, when she was weary of all the panoply of power. Inasfar as any imperial monument can be humble, this was humble. There are no portraits of her, no claims to divine protection. Instead there is a small blue cave, faintly lit by the honey-colored light coming through alabaster windows, with wheeling stars gleaming overhead, with the shapes of Christ and the apostles looming through the ghostly blue of space.

There are few buildings which are completely perfect, but this is one of them. The mausoleum is so small that it could easily be contained in a fairly large room, but although it is only forty feet long it gives an impression of immensity, of all space. The stars are not pinpoints of light but immense mosaic petals always eight-sided and formed of abstract shapes of red, white, gold, and apple-green, so designed that they seem to be moving out of the deep midnight blue, advancing and receding, never still. They are eyes and flowers; they melt and glow in a mysterious submarine light; heaven becomes a garden. On the dark blue dome a glimmering silver cross is outlined, and high up on the walls, like clouds, can be seen the apostles glowing in their white robes, while a youthful Christ tends His sheep.

It is best to enter the mausoleum without a guide, who will inevitably shine his flashlight on the mosaics and break the spell by draining away the richness of the colors, those intense blues and unearthly whites. The light from the thick alabaster windows is enough; and as the eye grows accustomed to the haunting shapes in the blue tomb, seeing the deer drinking at the well and the white doves beside the jets of holy water and the apostles blessing the dome of heaven, there comes inevitably the sensation of an infinite wheeling space, and if you stretch out your hand there will be no wall, and if you rise on tiptoe you will find yourself floating in the blue lake of heaven.

There are three tombs in the mausoleum, all of them of Greek marble. The central tomb contains the ashes of the Empress Galla Placidia, and was once covered with sheets of silver. For eleven centuries it remained undisturbed, with the embalmed body of the Empress sitting upright in a chair of cypress, arrayed in royal robes and wearing the tiara. We are told that in the sixteenth century it was one of the sights of Ravenna to peep through a little hole in the back of the tomb and see the changeless queen. In 1577 some careless children thrust a taper through the hole in the hope of seeing her more clearly. Crowding and pushing, watching excitedly at the hole, they brought the lighted taper too close to her, and in a moment the royal robes, the cypress chair, and the long-dead queen burst into flame, and in a few minutes there was nothing left but a small heap of ashes.

The mausoleum of Galla Placidia achieves its effect by a deliberate muting of light and by the invention of a hitherto unknown dimension of the color blue. The octagonal church of San Vitale, built a hundred years later in the reign of the Emperor Justinian, achieves its effect by a deliberate explosion of light and by the invention of hitherto unknown juxtapositions of color, by a boldness and fluency which mock the static grandeur of Byzantine art as it was practiced in Greece. Everything is in movement; the colors are sent clashing and reverberating through that octagonal chamber with its eight immense pillars. Gold, white, scarlet, and green—the colors of a summer afternoon—predominate. We are as far as we can possibly be from the midnight blue of Galla Placidia's mausoleum.

The church of San Vitale is only a hundred yards away from the mausoleum, but it could be on another continent. Once the entire interior was covered with mosaics, and so it might have remained if Charlemagne in his progress through Italy had not taken a delight in it, carrying its treasures away to ornament his palace church in Aachen. Today only the mosaics in the sanctuary survive to testify to the vigor and magnificence of the Slavic chieftain who adopted the name of Justinian. He had already built Hagia Sophia in Constantinople, and a host of other churches in the imperial capital. Now in this provincial capital he presents himself once more as the great architect who has bequeathed to Christianity a new and more splendid conception of its own destiny.

So he appears in the great mosaic on the choir which shows him surrounded by guards, imperial dignitaries, and bishops in the act of offering a golden *paten* to the church, symbolizing the great wealth he had expended on the cultivation of Christian magnificence. He already includes himself among the saints, for he wears a nimbus of gold and silver, the silver now faded into a dusty gray. He appears in all the panoply of his imperial dignity, in purple gown and red buskins, wearing a triple tiara of pearls, emeralds, and rubies, his hair brushed forward in the traditional manner of a Roman emperor, his fleshy face and steely eyes so faithfully recorded that it is clearly a portrait taken from life. He appears as a voluptuary, skilled in the enjoyment of his own extravagance, alert, intelligent, aware of his power and majesty, the knowledge that he has only to make a gesture and men will tremble for their lives.

In the history of Christian mosaics this panel, and the corresponding panel showing the Empress Theodora accompanied by her retinue, have a special importance, for something quite new has been added, not only in the use of daring colors and the sharp modulation of features by a technique as precise and carefully contrived as the flat planes of solid color used by Cézanne, but also in the use of the forgotten third dimension. There is depth in this portrait of the emperor attended by his courtiers and bishops. The air blows through the mosaic, the gowns rustle, the alert figures are about to step out into the space which lies in front of them. Their faces are still outlined against the hieratic gold of an eternal heaven, but their feet walk on a green and springing grass. They live in the elevated imperial world which is neither heaven nor earth, a world where everything is subtly larger than life and more intensely colored. In this world God is absent, for all authority derives from the emperor.

All the mosaics of San Vitale have this inner excitement, the insistent clang of color. The church was not built for midnight masses but for the streaming daylight; nor in a real sense was it a church, for it was intended to celebrate Justinian more than Christ. We see Moses pasturing the flock of his father-in-law, Jethro, and removing his sandals as he approaches the burning bush in a landscape where all the rocks emit mysterious fires, and then a hand appears from heaven, offering him the table of the law, which appears in the form of a rolled up imperial rescript, very small and very narrow; and the reason for depicting Moses in the mosaics is a very simple one—like Justinian, he was a great law-giver. Moses and Justinian wear the same features, and the Hebrew law-giver who never saw the promised land is regarded as the precursor of the emperor who conquered the land and assumed the power which goes with possession. Just as Galla Placidia erected a church to her own glory and dedicated it to Saint John the Evangelist, so Justinian erected the church to his own glory and dedicated it to Saint Vitalis.

There is very little religious feeling in the church: it is too sumptuous, too elegant, too decorative to permit the invasion of prayers. It is a place for intricate courtly dances, with the emperor or governor gazing down on the dancers from the gallery; and indeed the throne must have been in the gallery, for we know that Charlemagne placed his throne in the gallery of his palace church at Aachen, which was modeled closely on San Vitale. The sumptuous elegance applies even to the mystic Lamb, standing in a wreath set in an embroidered heaven of vines. The Lamb resembles a lapdog, and the decorative heaven might be the adornment of an empress's boudoir. By a curious and deliberate irony only the Empress Theodora, the harlot raised to the purple, wears a look of sanctity. With her cruel mouth, her marble pallor, her staring green-rimmed eyes with their exaggerated gaze of other-worldly contemplation, she might be a saint in ecstasy; but what she is ecstatic about is her own majesty. The hem of her robe is embroidered in gold with the three Magi bearing gifts for the Christ child and kneeling in adoration, but the empress herself does not bend her knees. This portrait, too, must have been made from life.

The church of San Vitale was consecrated in A.D. 547 and the same year saw the consecration of the church of Sant' Apollinare in Classe on the outskirts of the city and looking out on the teeming port. Where San Vitale expresses the glorification of an emperor, this church expresses the glorification of Saint Apollinaris, the patron saint of Ravenna, who was martyred on this spot and buried in the crypt. A deep religious feeling fills the interior. A golden cross arises in a starlit sky in the apse, while Christ looks down on Elijah and Moses, and there are three lambs representing the three apostles who were present at the Transfiguration on Mount Tabor. Saint Apollinaris, in the classic posture of an *orans* with uplifted hands, stands beneath the cross while twelve more lambs, representing the apostles or the tribes of Israel, walk with him through the gardens of Paradise. Strange rocks and tufts of flowers lie about the garden; the sun of heaven shines; the smallest flowers throw their blue shadows.

The vision of Paradise was never so brilliantly expressed in mosaics. Not even in the rotunda of Saint George at Salonika, where the saints stand before the jeweled walls of the heavenly Jerusalem, is there the sense of a *habitable* heaven, a pleasure garden for the saints, a meadow sanctified by God's peace. The sheep—there are altogether twenty-seven of them, for there are twelve more on the triumphal arch above the apse—

are not the familiar sheep we see every day. They move gracefully and delicately, and look a little like white borzois; they, too, have been "made perfect." Below the apse are five windows; the sun pours through them and throws its reflected light on the mosaics above. This, too, is a novel invention, and the use of this undercutting, upward-flowing light is rarely found in later churches. In ancient days the entire floor and perhaps all the walls were covered with mosaics, and the effect must have been almost too sumptuous. Today only the apse, the triumphal arch, and the walls between the windows are covered with them—to the advantage of the observer, who can concentrate on the majesty in front of him without being distracted by majesty on all sides.

In time the relics of Saint Apollinaris were removed for greater safety to another church within the city walls, which was henceforth called Sant' Apollinare Nuovo. It was not a new church, for it was built during the reign of Theodoric, the king of the Goths, whose red-roofed palace with fluttering curtains appears on the mosaics. Under Justinian the three banks of mosaics were subtly altered, and there is some evidence to suggest that the great processions of martyred saints, the men on one side and the women of the other, belong to his reign. The men in their white gowns and the women in their jewel-colored robes march to some stately music through the fields of Paradise to receive their reward at the hands of the Virgin and the Christ child. Their names are written above them—Vincentia, Valeria, Crispina, Lucia. . . . In the shadow of the date palms they walk through the flowering fields.

Four angels guard the Virgin; the three Magi make their offerings; the march of the saints continues around the walls from the earthly palace of Theodoric to the heavenly throne of the Virgin. Each saint has an individual and recognizable face, and all, or nearly all, hide their hands modestly in their gowns, as though they dare not touch the crowns of martyrdom not yet blessed by Christ. The women wear the ornate costumes of the Byzantine court, while the men appear dressed in the gowns of Roman senators.

What is remarkable is the harmony of this long liturgical procession, the sense of movement flowing through them, as though they were being impelled forward not by the motion of their legs and bodies but with an immaterial divine energy. They glide in the winds of heaven, hover in divinity, hurl themselves headlong toward the Virgin's throne without seeming to move at all. Almost the same effect is produced by the Parthenon frieze, where the young riders move and do not move, caught in a moment of eternity.

As Salonika contains the greatest treasure chest of mosaics in Greece, so Ravenna contains the greatest in Italy. All over Italy, and especially in Rome and Venice, you will come across mosaics, but never in such a quantity, designed with so much grace and dexterity. The mosaics of Ravenna were constructed by court artists, and they have the delicacy and power which comes only from men trained in the narrow, luxurious traditions of the court. Most of the Roman mosaics have a somber quality: the lightning is always about to strike, Christ and the apostles are caught in moments of rigidity; dark shadows move across the face of the heavens. The great illuminated mosaic cross at San Clemente in Rome, with the white doves shining like altar lamps beside it, has something of the quality of the apse at Sant' Apollinare in Classe; the Virgin at Torcello, and the lesser known and even more beautiful Virgin at Murano, stand with a divine authority; there are details here and there in Saint Mark's in Venice which derive from Byzantine masters; the Christ of SS. Cosma e Damiano in Rome is a figure of triumphant power; but the crown remains in Ravenna.

That ancient art has had its consummation. Never again can we hope to see the mosaic masters of Byzantium creating their "monuments of unaging intellect." We no longer know the secret of making divine excitement out of cool dispassionate stones and chips of glass; we can more easily fly to the moon than create another Hagia Sophia or another church of the Virgin of the Golden Laurels. By the time of Dante the thousand-year-old tradition was coming to an end, and a new energy, a new purpose was moving through Christianity, and in the process something very precious was being lost.

So we return to our own world, where the stillness of the light is absent and the colors of a visionary heaven are rarely displayed, where mortality confronts us everlast-ingly and we are no longer so deeply moved by the everlasting promise of peace which the mosaic masters painted on the walls. We return at last to the familiar world which Yeats described in the opening verse of "Sailing to Byzantium":

> That is no country for old men. The young
> In one another's arms, birds in the trees,
> —Those dying generations—at their song,
> The salmon-falls, the mackerel-crowded seas.
> Fish, flesh, or fowl, commend all summer long
> Whatever is begotten, born, and dies.
> Caught in that sensual music all neglect
> Monuments of unaging intellect.

Plates